Totally WACKY FACTS ABOUT ANIMALS

CARI MEISTER

CAPSTONE PRESS
a capstone imprint

Vultures
PEE ON THEIR
LEGS to keep cool.
It's natural
AIR-CONDITIONING!

A hot crocodile sleeps with its mouth WIDE OPEN.

A turkey group is called a **POSSE**, and a peacock group is called a **PARTY**.

A group of kangaroos is called a **MOB**.

A flamingo flock can have up to **1.5 MILLION BIRDS!**

WATCH OUT! A group of rhinos is called a

CRASH.

THE CHICKEN IS CLOSELY RELATED TO TYRANNOSAURUS REX.

Why didn't I get those **HUGE TEETH?**

A chicken has a "COMB" on its head and two "WATTLES" under its neck.

Mike the Headless Chicken lived for 18 months without HIS HEAD!

Baby monkeys suck their THUMBS.

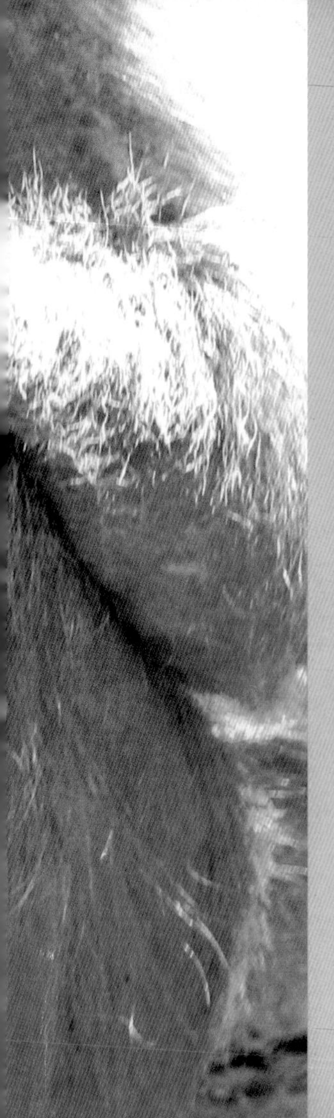

Baby elephants suck their TRUNKS.

Giraffes use their TONGUES to clean their EARS and NOSES.

Orangutans use their teeth to clip their toenails.
House cats spend 50% of their waking time GROOMING THEMSELVES.

Female REDBACK spiders EAT THEIR MATES.

Bald eagle partners stay together for a lifetime.

A CAPYBARA EATS ITS OWN POOP.
Pandas poop about 40 times per day!
I blame it on the BAMBOO.

SLOTHS POOP ONLY ONCE A WEEK.

I should try
EATING BAMBOO!

SOME HUMMINGBIRDS WEIGH LESS THAN A PENNY.

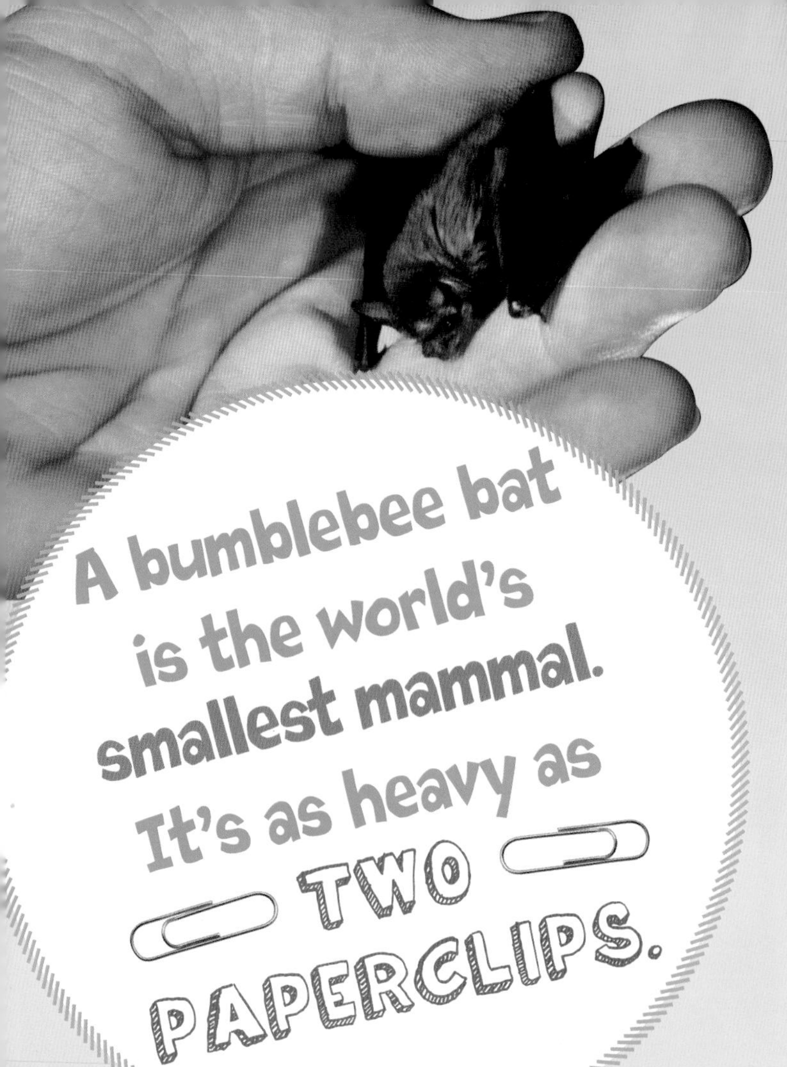

A bumblebee bat is the world's smallest mammal. It's as heavy as TWO PAPERCLIPS.

The world's smallest dog, a Chihuahua, can fit in a

1 SECOND:

THE TIME IT TAKES A TIGER BEETLE TO RUN **120 TIMES** ITS OWN BODY LENGTH

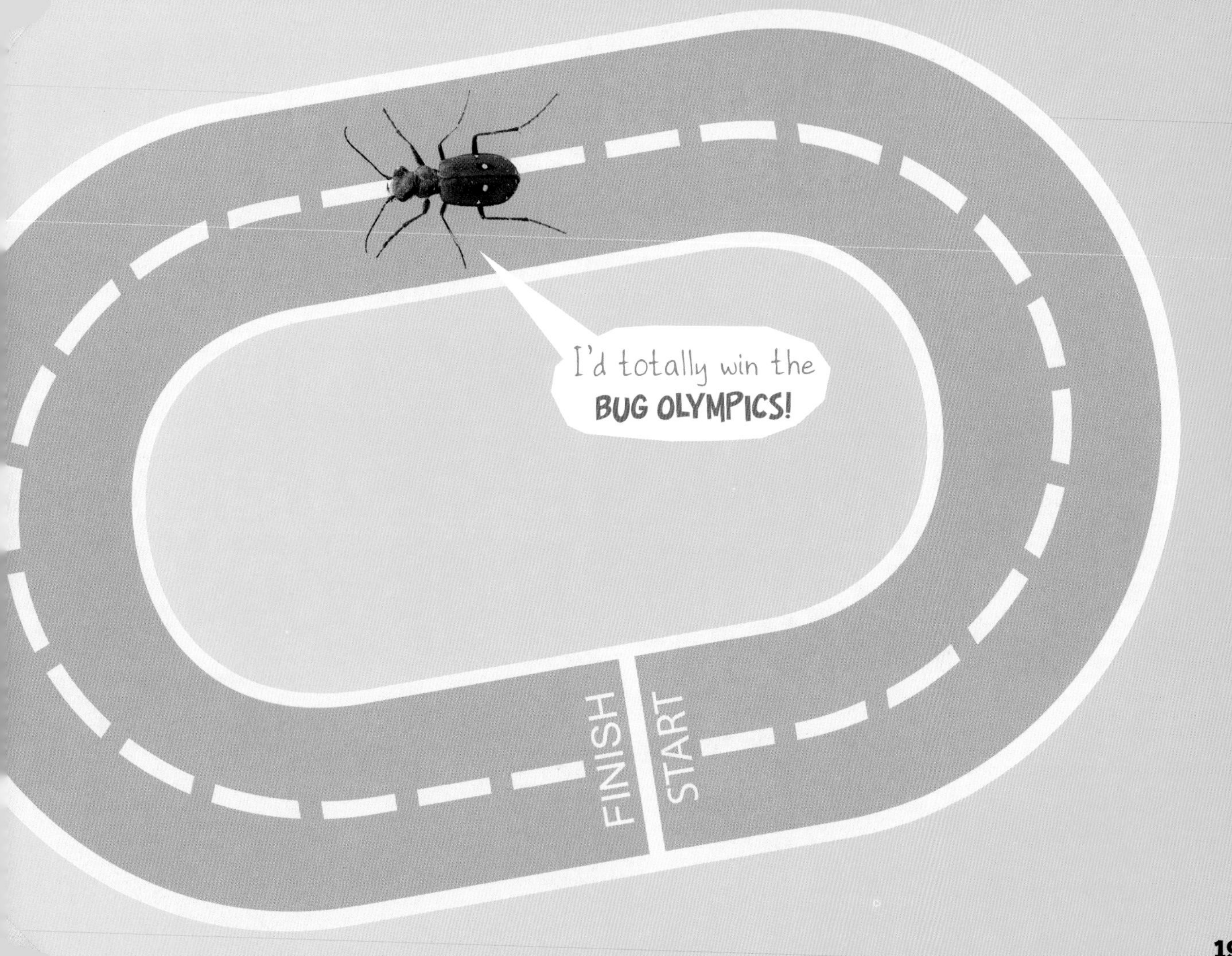
I'd totally win the
BUG OLYMPICS!
FINISH
START

The cheetah clocks in as the **fastest mammal**, running **70 miles (113 kilometers)** per hour.

The PEREGRINE FALCON can reach speeds of up to 200 MILES (322 km) PER HOUR!

Pit vipers can see INFRARED.

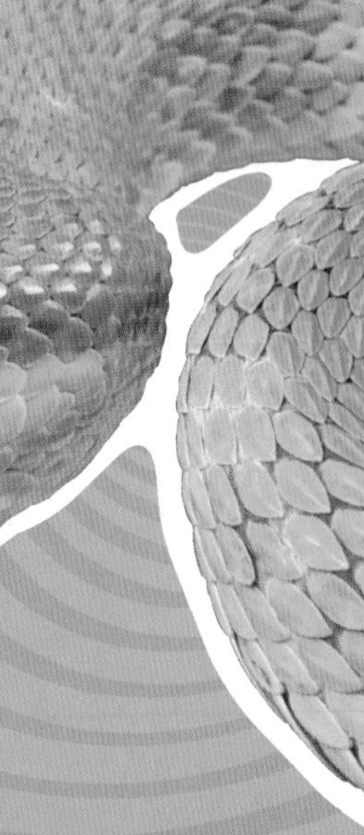

Rats have an uncanny ability to DETECT LAND MINES.

The greater wax moth can hear sounds at higher frequencies than any other animal.

The African drongo bird mimics a meerkat's warning call to steal MEERKAT FOOD.

A hawk moth caterpillar larva looks like **A SNAKE** to fool predators.

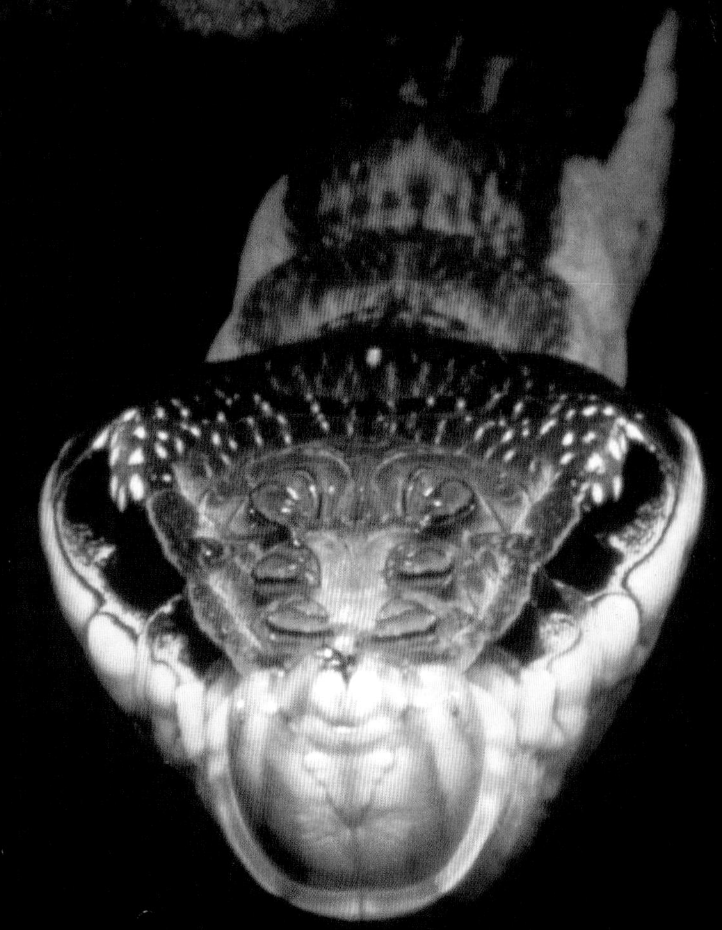

Male "dancing frogs" WAVE THEIR LEGS in the air to ATTRACT FEMALES.

A FEMALE SLUG sometimes bites off a male slug's PRIVATE PARTS.

Male porcupines PEE on females before mating.

HOGNOSE SNAKES

let out stinky "**death**" smells to avoid

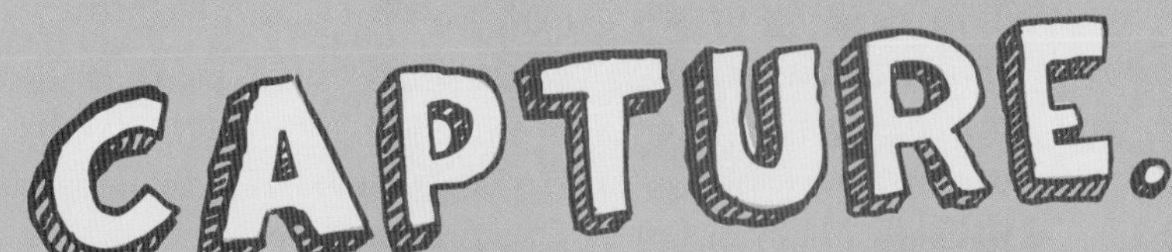

SOME DUCKS **PLAY DEAD** TO AVOID BECOMING A FOX'S MEAL.

An opossum will PLAY DEAD for hours, even sticking out its tongue for added effect.

Bees and butterflies drink CROCODILE TEARS.

SOME MOTHS HAVE HARPOON-SHAPED MOUTHPARTS TO SUCK TEARS FROM SLEEPING BIRDS.

Some kinds of carpenter ants purposely explode with TOXIC GOO to stop predators.

The Moroccan flic-flac spider BACK-HANDSPRINGS away from its enemies.

HIPPOS FLING POOP AT EACH OTHER WHEN GETTING OUT OF THE WATER.

Flies lay their eggs in rotting flesh.

A JACKAL CUB EATS ITS MAMA'S BARF.

TUSKS ARE REALLY VERY LARGE TEETH.

An elephant's tusks can grow to be 10 feet (3 meters) long.

A cow's
udder can
hold almost
6 GALLONS
(23 liters)
of milk.

Got an **upset stomach?** Try drinking

MOOSE MILK!

The giant African land snail has lots of teeth on its TONGUE!

An alligator can regrow one tooth 50 TIMES.

A vulture PUKES to keep enemies at bay.

FLIES EAT
POOP.

THE EMPEROR TAMARIN MONKEY HAS A LONG, BUSHY, WHITE MOUSTACHE!

You **KNOW** you want one too!

NO TWO TIGERS
HAVE THE
SAME STRIPES.

A zebra's
stripes keep
biting flies
AWAY.

WANT TO HAVE A SNOWBALL FIGHT?

JAPANESE MACAQUE MONKEYS WILL JOIN YOU!

And you thought I was **JUST CUTE.**

Millions of **monarch butterflies** migrate to the Monarch Butterfly Reserve in Mexico each fall. Trees there **BEND** with the weight of all of the butterflies!

Newborn elephants weigh about

200 POUNDS

(91 kilograms)!

A newborn hippo can weigh
110 POUNDS (50 kg).

EGYPTIAN VULTURES USE
ROCKS TO BREAK OPEN
OSTRICH EGGS.

The American burying beetle buries dead birds and rodents for its BABIES to eat.

ELEPHANTS ARE THE ONLY LAND MAMMALS THAT CAN'T JUMP.

A penguin can't fly, but it can JUMP 6 feet (1.8 m) in the air from the water!

The Australian striped rocket frog can jump over 4 FEET (1.2 M).

Kangaroos can't run, but they can travel 25 feet (7.6 m)
IN ONE LEAP.

THINK FARM ANIMALS ARE BORING?

MUSIC CALMS NERVOUS COWS.

One sheep produces enough wool in a year to make a man's suit.
PIGS CAN'T SWEAT. THEY ROLL IN MUD TO STAY COOL.

A dog named Chaser has learned to recognize more than 1,000 words.

CROWS MAY BE ABLE TO COUNT.

SOME ELEPHANTS CAN BE TRAINED
TO PAINT
SELF-PORTRAITS.

Rhino horns are made up of the same stuff as your HAIR.

THE NAKED MOLE RAT HAS NO HAIR.

Monkeys pick (and eat) BUGS out of each other's hair.

POLAR BEAR MAMAS GAIN **400 POUNDS (181 KG)** DURING PREGNANCY.

Mama crocodiles carry their babies around in their MOUTHS.

The yellow ant smells like a **LEMON.**

One kind of millipede smells like **CHERRY COLA.**

The hoatzin bird smells like **COW DUNG.**

A BINTURONG'S BEHIND SMELLS REMARKABLY LIKE BUTTERED POPCORN!
MOVIES, ANYONE?

RETICULATED PYTHONS CAN GROW AS LONG AS 32 FEET (9.8 M)!

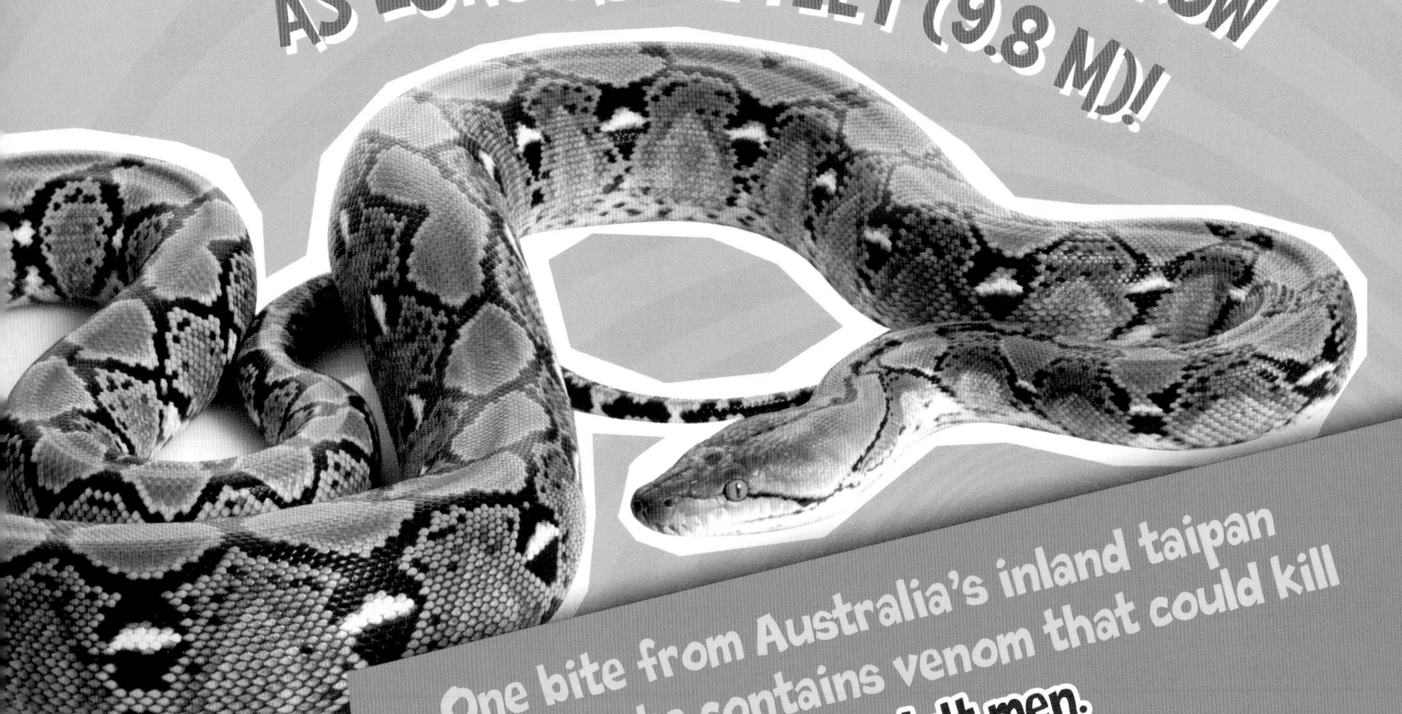

One bite from Australia's inland taipan snake contains venom that could kill **100 adult men.**

MANY SNAKES DISLOCATE THEIR JAWS SO THEY CAN SWALLOW LARGE ANIMALS WHOLE.

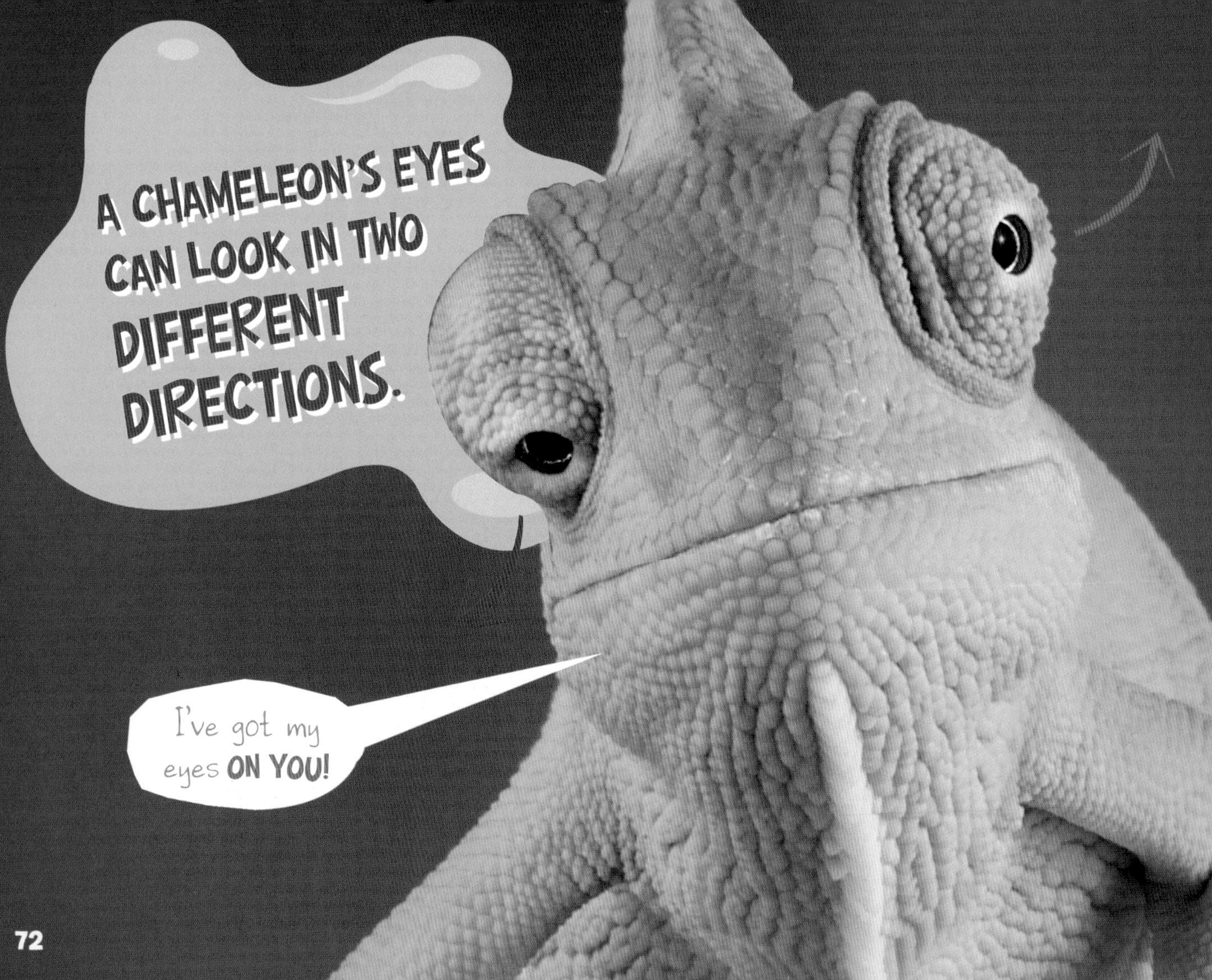
A CHAMELEON'S EYES CAN LOOK IN TWO DIFFERENT DIRECTIONS.
I've got my eyes ON YOU!

The horned lizard can shoot BLOOD out of its eyes.

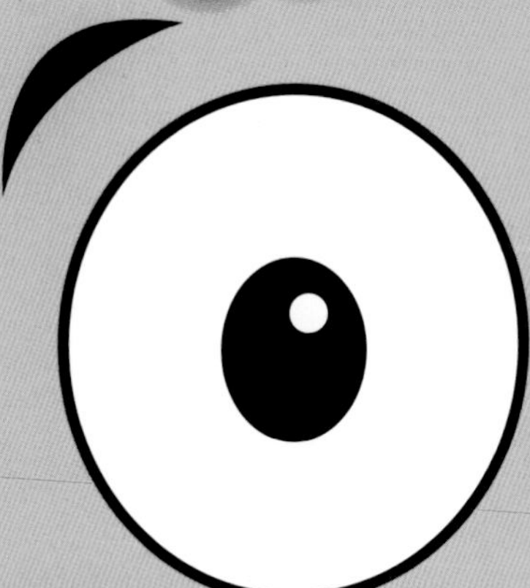

SNAKES DO NOT BLINK.

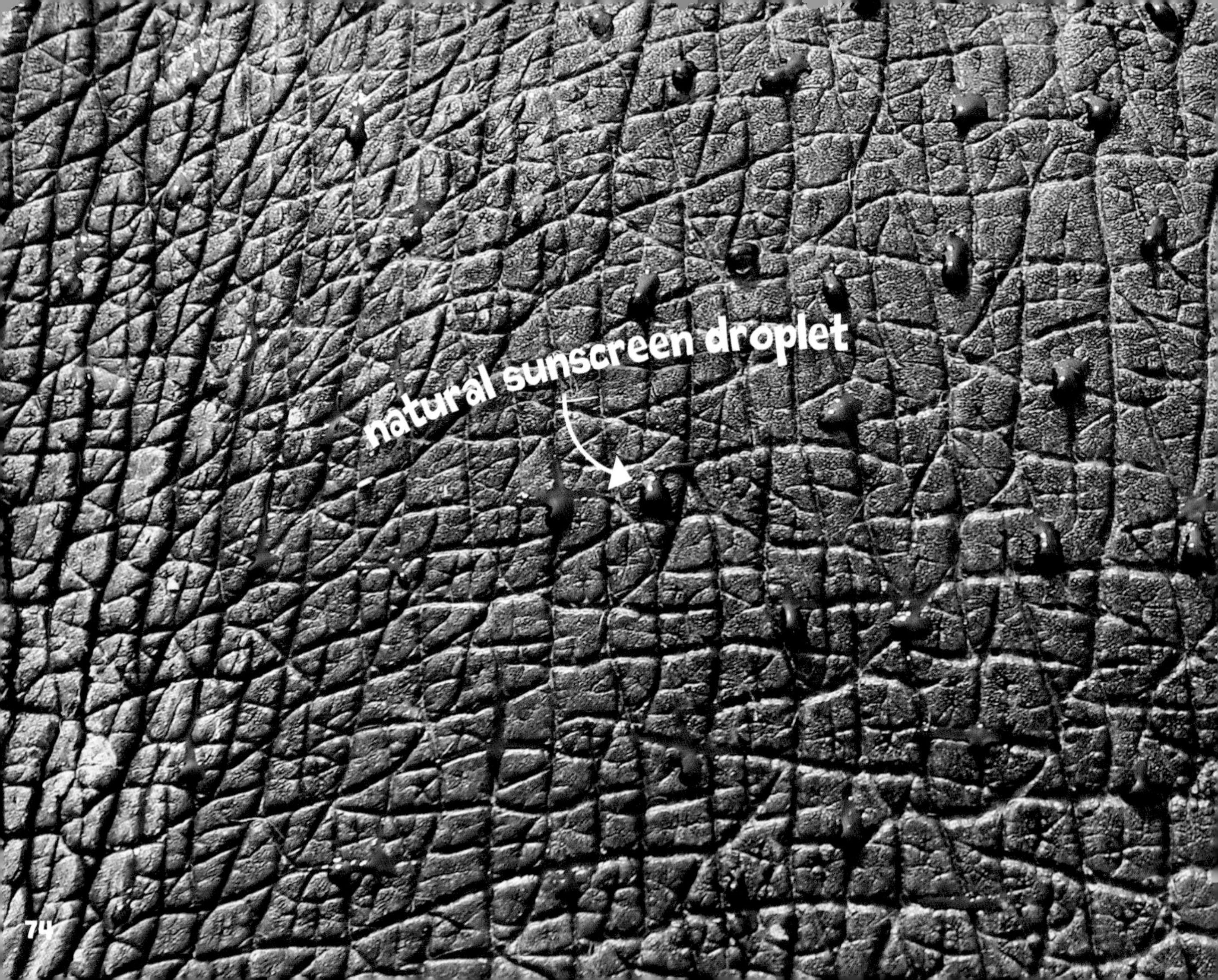
natural sunscreen droplet

A HIPPO'S SWEAT
ACTS AS A
SUNSCREEN AND
INSECT REPELLENT.

Geckos can **REGROW** their tails.

If a flatworm is
cut in half,
each piece will
grow into a new worm.

RIP

TWO DAYS AFTER AN ANT DIES, OTHER ANTS CARRY IT AWAY TO AN

ANT GRAVEYARD.

RHINOS COVER
THEMSELVES IN MUD
TO KEEP BUGS AWAY.

Polar bears have BLACK SKIN.

Like its fur, a tiger's skin is STRIPED.

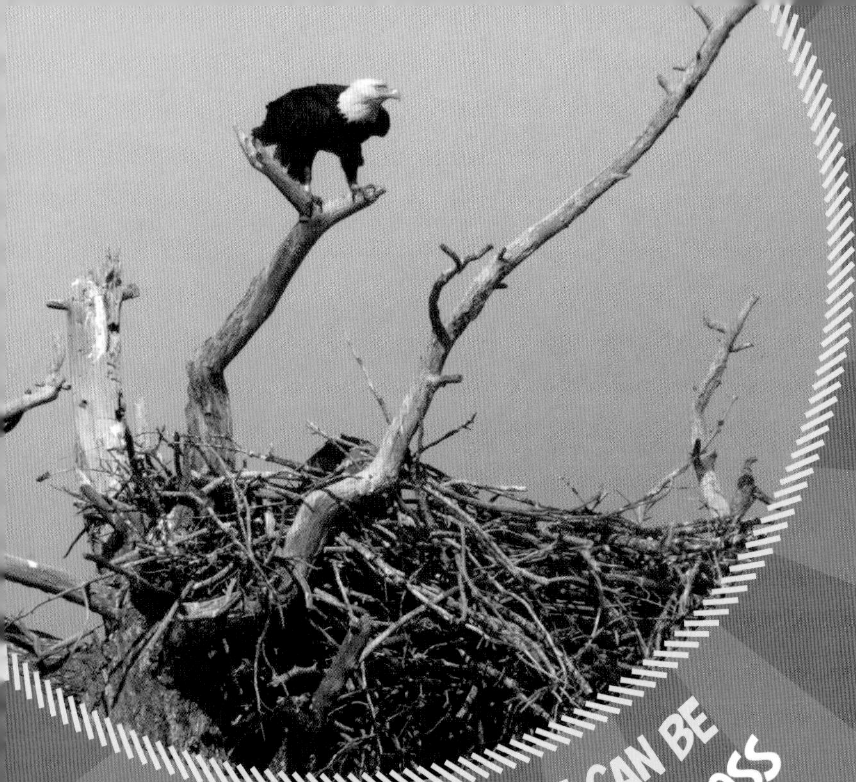

A BALD EAGLE'S NEST CAN BE MORE THAN 9 FEET (2.7 M) ACROSS AND 20 FEET (6 M) TALL.

An edible-nest swiftlet makes its nest out of SPIT.

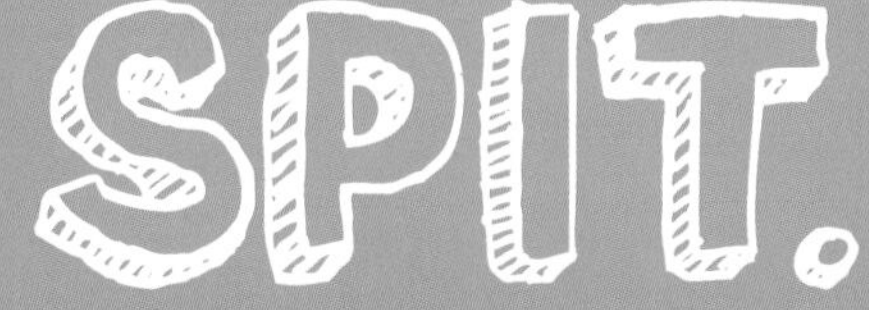

SOCIABLE WEAVERS BUILD MASSIVE NESTS THAT HOUSE 400 BIRDS.

Female American sand burrowing mayflies live for **less than 5 minutes.**

GALAPAGOS TORTOISES CAN LIVE TO BE 150 YEARS OLD.

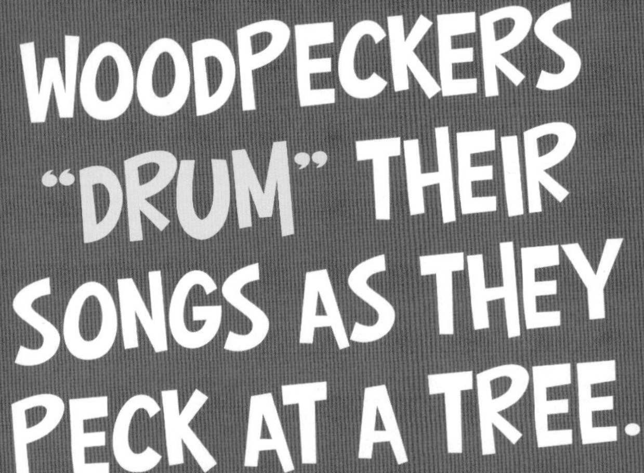

HOUSEFLIES HUM IN THE KEY OF F!

A red-eyed vireo sings 20,000 songs per day.

That's more songs than you have on **YOUR MP3 PLAYER!**

Giraffes sleep
with their eyes
HALF OPEN.

HORSES, ZEBRAS, AND ELEPHANTS SLEEP STANDING UP.

A CAT'S EAR HAS 32 MUSCLES;
A HUMAN'S EAR HAS TWO.

100,000:
the number of muscles
in an elephant's trunk

OWLS SWALLOW THEIR FOOD WHOLE AND THEN COUGH UP PELLETS OF BONES AND FUR.

Blister beetles release a chemical
used to treat human warts.

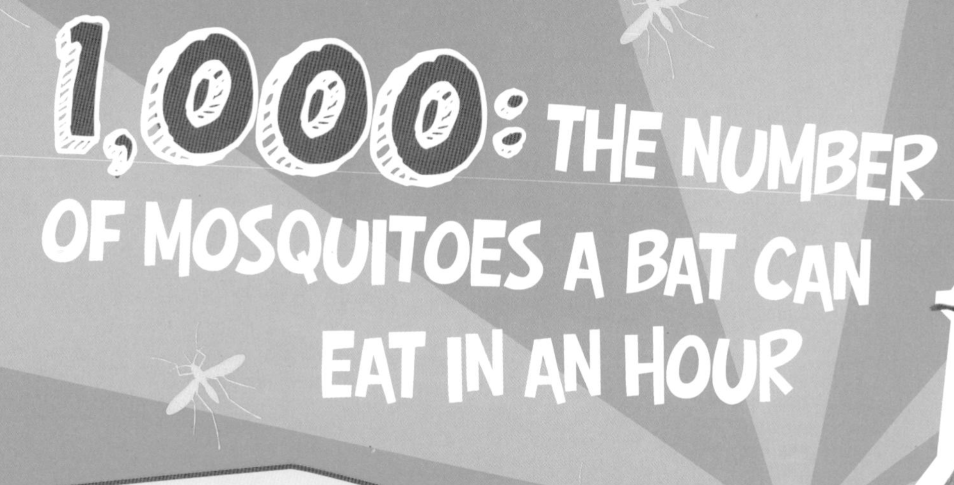

1,000: THE NUMBER OF MOSQUITOES A BAT CAN EAT IN AN HOUR

Insects have been on Earth for about 400 million years.

A kind of skink lizard has

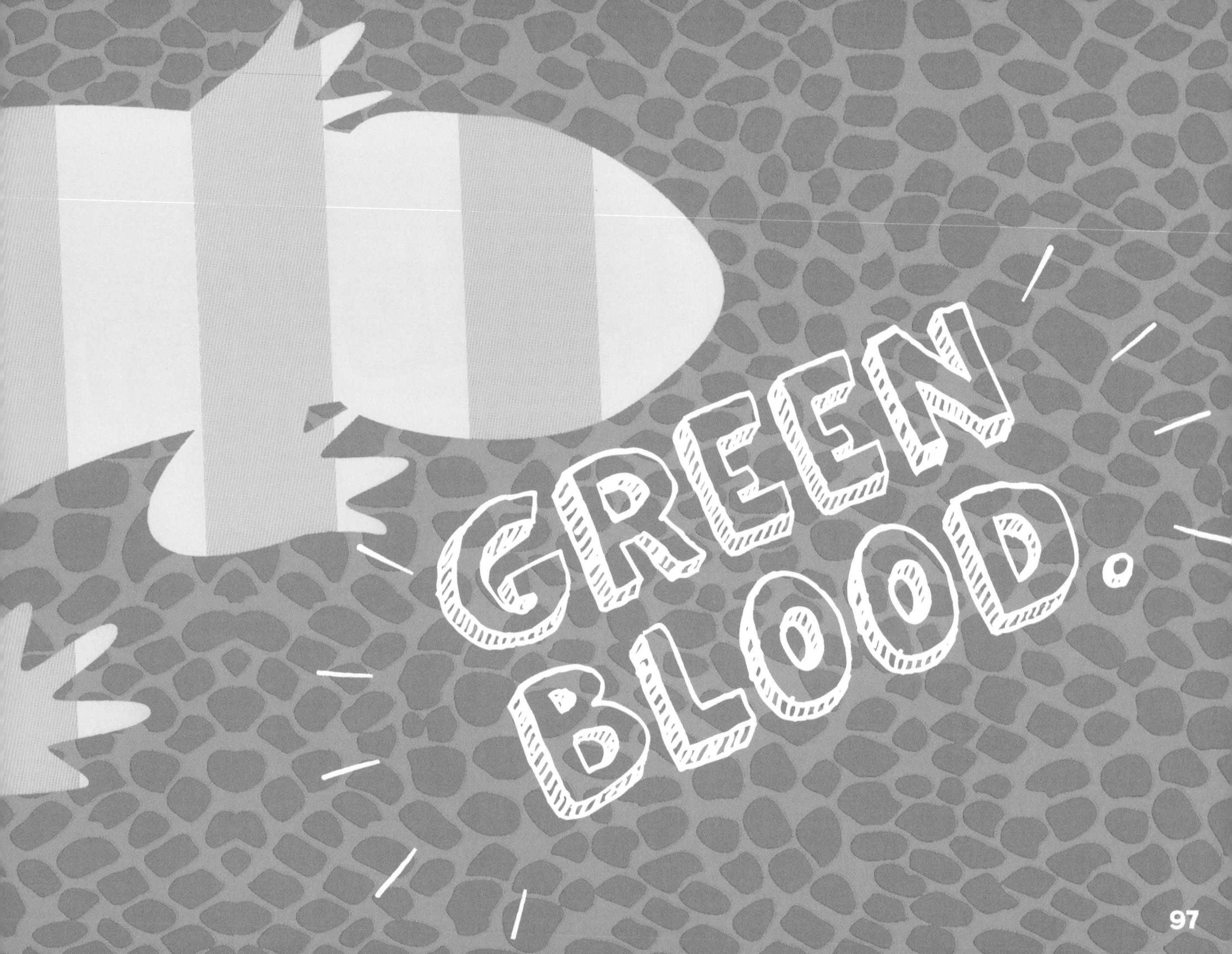
GREEN
BLOOD.

A millipede can have up to 750 legs.

A CATERPILLAR HAS 16 LEGS.

A TARSIER'S EYE IS BIGGER THAN ITS BRAIN.
Most spiders have four sets of eyes.

DRAGONFLIES HAVE 360-DEGREE VISION.

I CAN SEE YOU!

Female mandrill monkeys like males with brightly colored **behinds and faces.**

MALE FRIGATE BIRDS INFLATE THEIR HUGE, RED NECK POUCH TO
ATTRACT FEMALES.

I think I can fit ONE MORE.

A chipmunk's cheek pouches can hold about 32 beechnuts.

A mole can dig a tunnel that's 300 feet (91 m) long in about 20 HOURS.

ONE UNDERGROUND PRAIRIE DOG TOWN COVERED

SQUARE MILES (64,750 SQUARE KM)!

THERE ARE **TWO** SPECIES OF ELEPHANTS IN THE WORLD.

FOUR KINDS OF ANTEATERS EXIST.

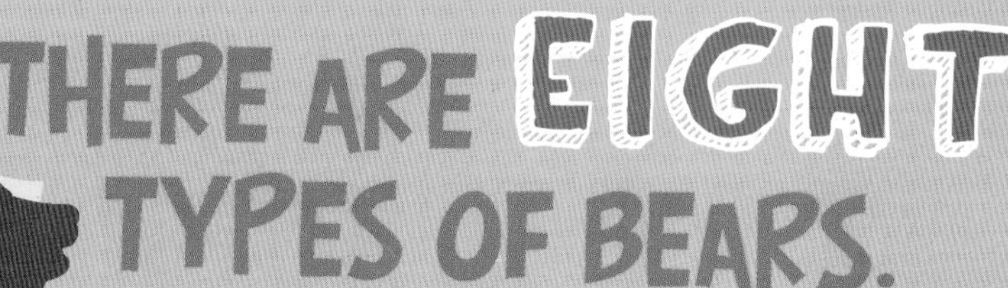

THERE ARE **EIGHT** TYPES OF BEARS.

AND MORE THAN **1.5 MILLION** KINDS OF INSECTS HAVE BEEN NAMED IN THE WORLD!

MOOSE KILL MORE PEOPLE THAN GRIZZLY BEARS.

A MAN IS 90% MORE LIKELY THAN A WOMAN TO BE ATTACKED BY A GREAT WHITE SHARK.

Um, can I pretend to be a **WOMAN?**

GORILLAS can catch a HUMAN COLD.

AHH-CHOO!

BUBONIC PLAGUE IS SPREAD BY FLEAS.

WHEN DANGER

Kangaroos THUMP their FEET.

Beavers slap their TAILS against the WATER.

Ants let out "perfume" from their antennae to signal danger.

IS NEAR ...

Hyenas make LOW ALARM RUMBLES.

DESPITE BEING CATS, JAGUARS LIKE TO SWIM.

The black panther is really just a BLACK LEOPARD.

LIONS ARE THE ONLY BIG CATS THAT LIVE IN GROUPS.

EACH WEEK THREE NEW MARINE SPECIES ARE DISCOVERED.

There are more than 200 different species of stingrays.

THERE ARE OVER 16,000 DIFFERENT KINDS OF OCEAN FISH.

There are seven
kinds of sea turtles.

A tiger pistol shrimp's snapping claw is louder than a jet engine.

Great white sharks can smell blood from 3 miles (4.8 km) away.

A SEAL'S WHISKERS CAN SENSE A FISH SWIMMING 600 FEET (183 M) AWAY.
Just call me MR. SENSITIVE.

A VIPERFISH HAS FANGS SO LONG THAT THEY DON'T FIT IN ITS MOUTH.

ONE KIND OF DEEP-SEA SQUID HAS LIPS THAT LOOK LIKE HUMAN TEETH.

ELECTRIC EELS create up to 600 VOLTS of electricity—enough to shock a person to death!

The snapping shrimp uses one of its claws as a WATER PISTOL.

A mantis shrimp can punch with the force of a moving bullet.

THE LARGEST FISH IN THE SEA, THE WHALE SHARK, IS LONGER THAN A SCHOOL BUS.

A bull shark can weigh almost as much as a **grand piano.**

6 FEET (1.8 M): THE HEIGHT OF A MALE ORCA'S DORSAL FIN

The ocean sunfish can weigh up to 5,000 pounds (2,268 kg).

The Japanese spider crab can measure 12 feet (3.7 m) from claw to claw!

SNAKEHEAD FISH CAN SURVIVE OUT OF WATER FOR UP TO FOUR DAYS.

DOLPHINS

work together to bring an injured dolphin to the water's surface to BREATHE.

If an OCTOPUS loses an arm, a new one grows.
Pretty HANDY, huh?

SEA CREATURES THAT CAN CHANGE THEIR GENDER:

anemone fish

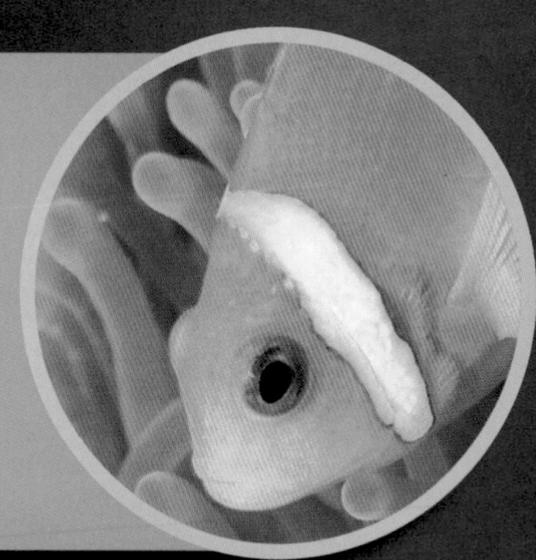

parrotfish

hawkfish

Check out SPERM WHALES!

A SPERM WHALE'S BRAIN IS **5 TIMES LARGER** THAN A HUMAN'S.

You're jealous, **RIGHT?**

A sperm whale can hold its breath for up to

90

MINUTES.

A sperm whale eats about

1 TON

(0.89 metric tons) of squid, octopuses, and fish in a single day!

ONE KIND OF ICEFISH HAS **CLEAR BLOOD.**

STARFISH HAVE NO BLOOD.

Who needs **BLOOD**, anyway?

Octopuses, lobsters, and squid
have blue blood.

A colossal squid's eye is the size of a

SOME LOBSTERS ARE COMPLETELY BLIND.

THE PEANUT WORM CAN PULL ITS HEAD (INCLUDING TENTACLES) INSIDE ITS BODY.

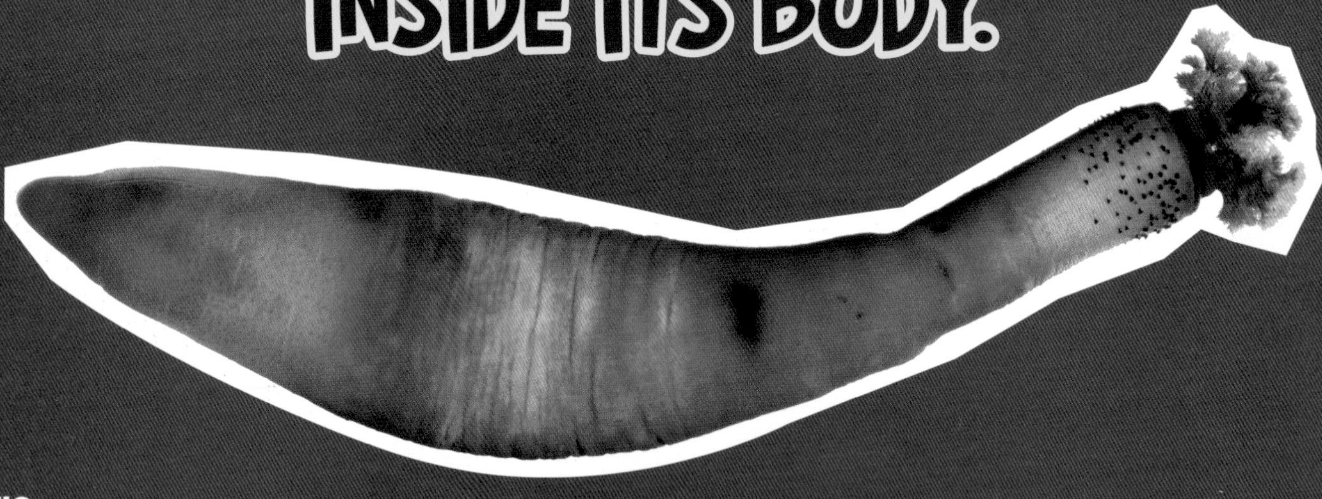

A sun jellyfish has poisonous tentacles that are more than 200 feet (61 m) long.

Sea lions have great eyesight, so the U.S. military trains them to find equipment lost at sea.

DOLPHINS use sonar to find UNDERWATER MINES for the U.S. military.

Sponges have no BRAINS, but they do sneeze, and it lasts as long as ONE HOUR!

Firefly squid have hundreds of blue flashing lights.

DEEP-SEA DRAGONFISH WAVE AROUND A LIGHTED BARBEL TO ATTRACT FOOD.

Lantern sharks glow in the DARK.

WHOSE HEARTBEAT?

A blue whale's heart beats only 8–10 times per minute.

MANATEES: 40–80 BEATS PER MINUTE

Antarctic fur seals:
110 beats per minute

Dinosaurs ate sawfish.

What **DIDN'T** I eat?

SHARKS ARE OLDER THAN DINOSAURS!

Scientists think coelacanths have been around for 300 MILLION YEARS.

FLYING FISH USE THEIR DORSAL FINS TO GLIDE THROUGH THE AIR.

Great white sharks can launch themselves 8–10 feet (2.4–3 m) into the air.

WHAT IS IT?

A MIMIC OCTOPUS CAN CHANGE ITS SHAPE AND COLOR TO LOOK LIKE A LION FISH.

A vampire squid

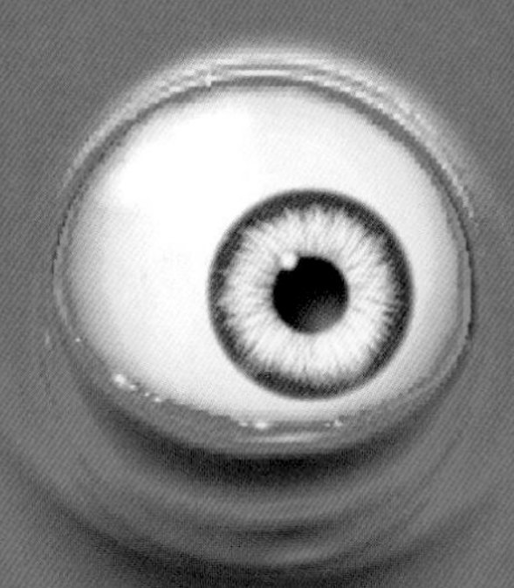

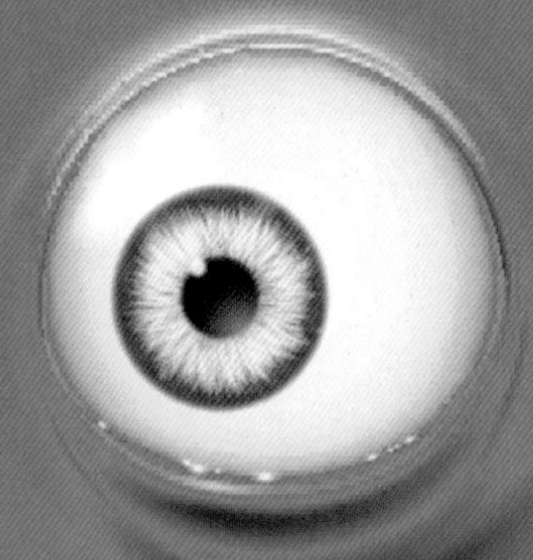

has red eyes.

Some see-through shrimp hitch rides on see-through jellyfish.

The glass squid has polka dots.

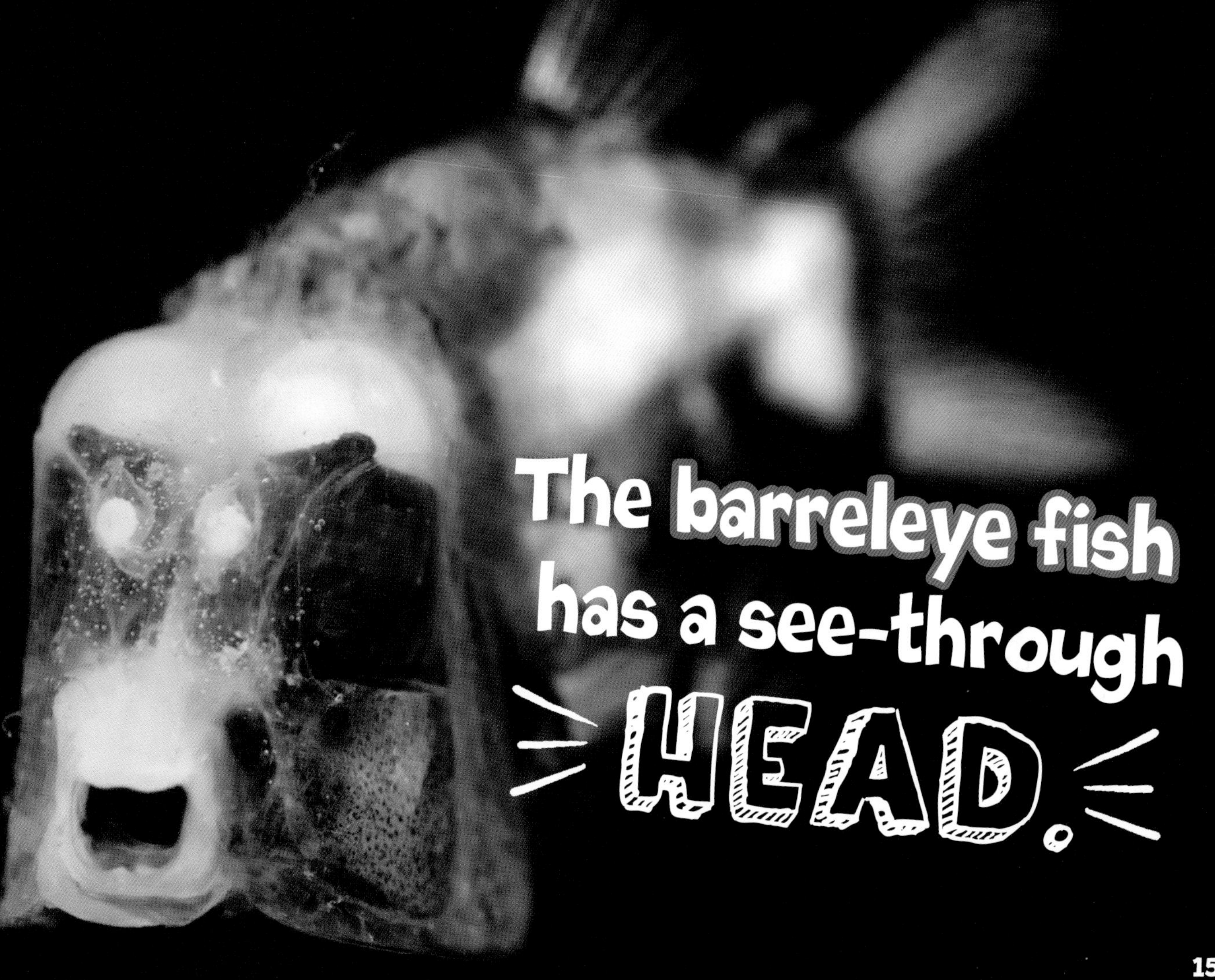
The barreleye fish
has a see-through
HEAD.

Pink handfish use their front fins to walk on the sea floor.

The tripod fish props itself up on two fins to **stand** on the ocean floor.

Octopuses taste food with suction cups that line each of their arms.

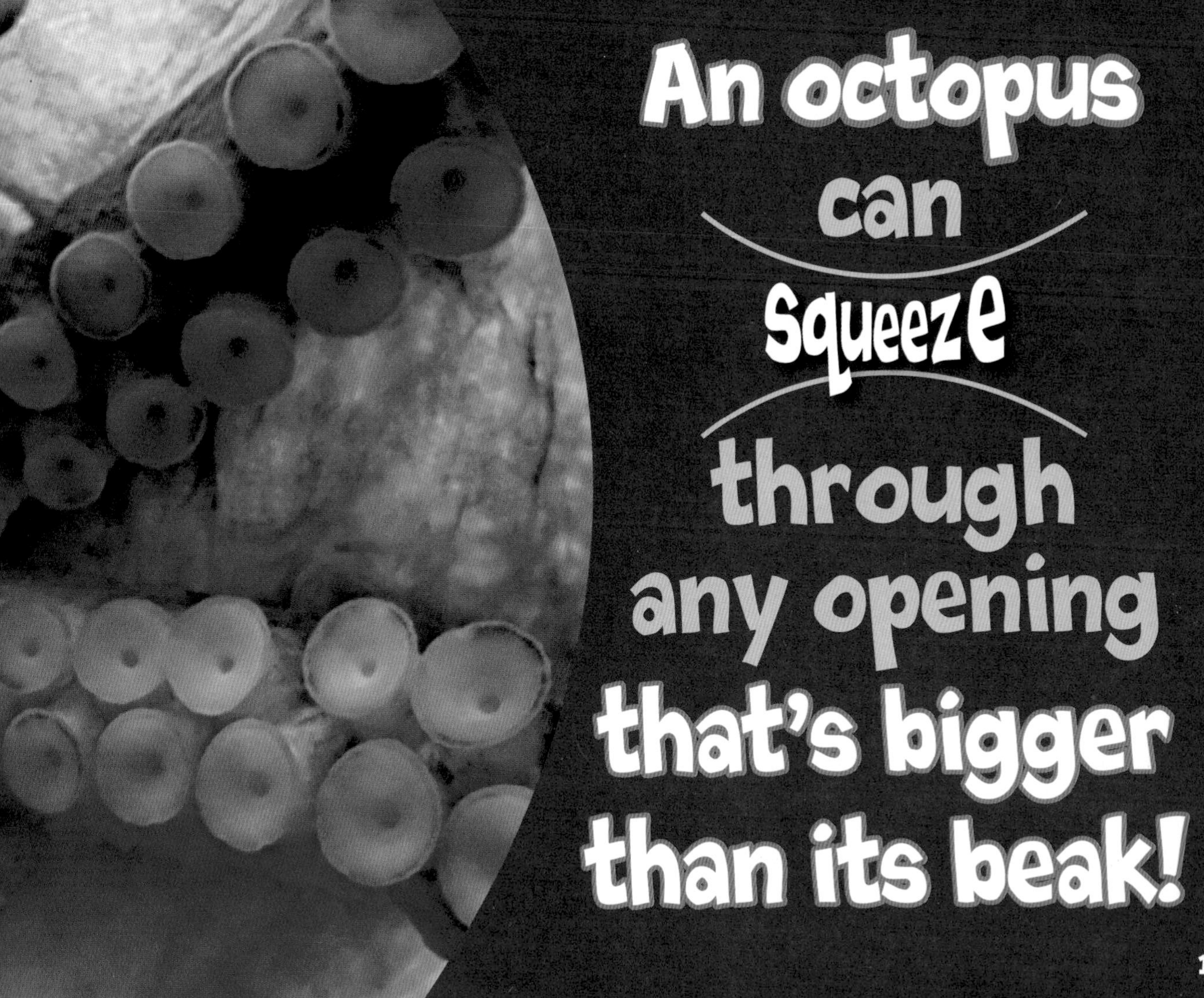
An octopus
can
squeeze
through
any opening
that's bigger
than its beak!

A blue whale is about 25 feet (7.6 m) long when it's born.

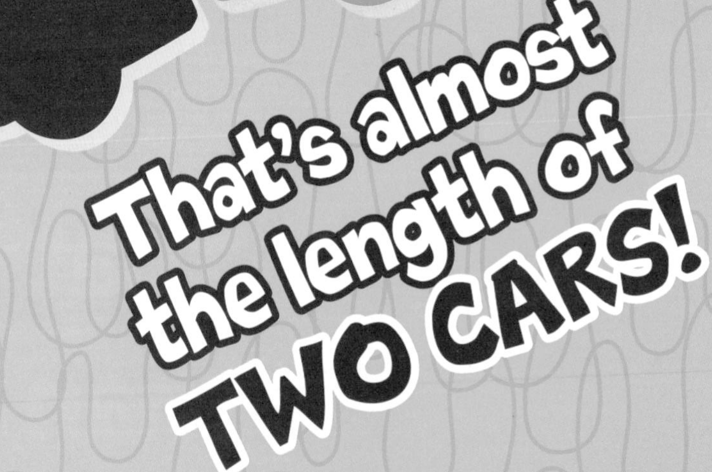

1 JELLY BEAN = the size of a newborn sea horse

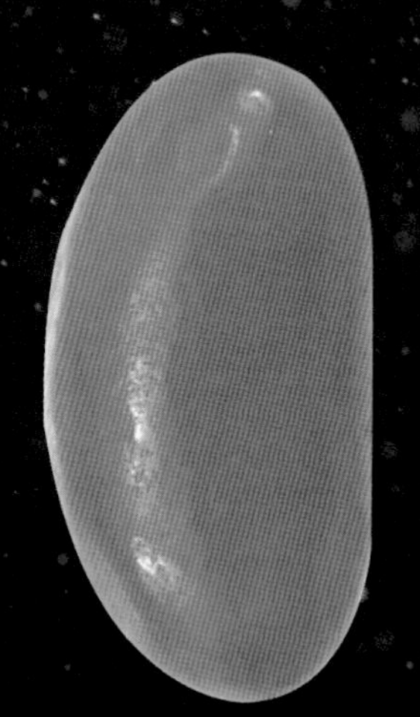

Some sea cucumbers look like poop.

Cleaner wrasses eat infections off of other fish.

PEOPLE USE OILY LUMPS FROM A WHALE'S STOMACH TO MAKE PERFUME.

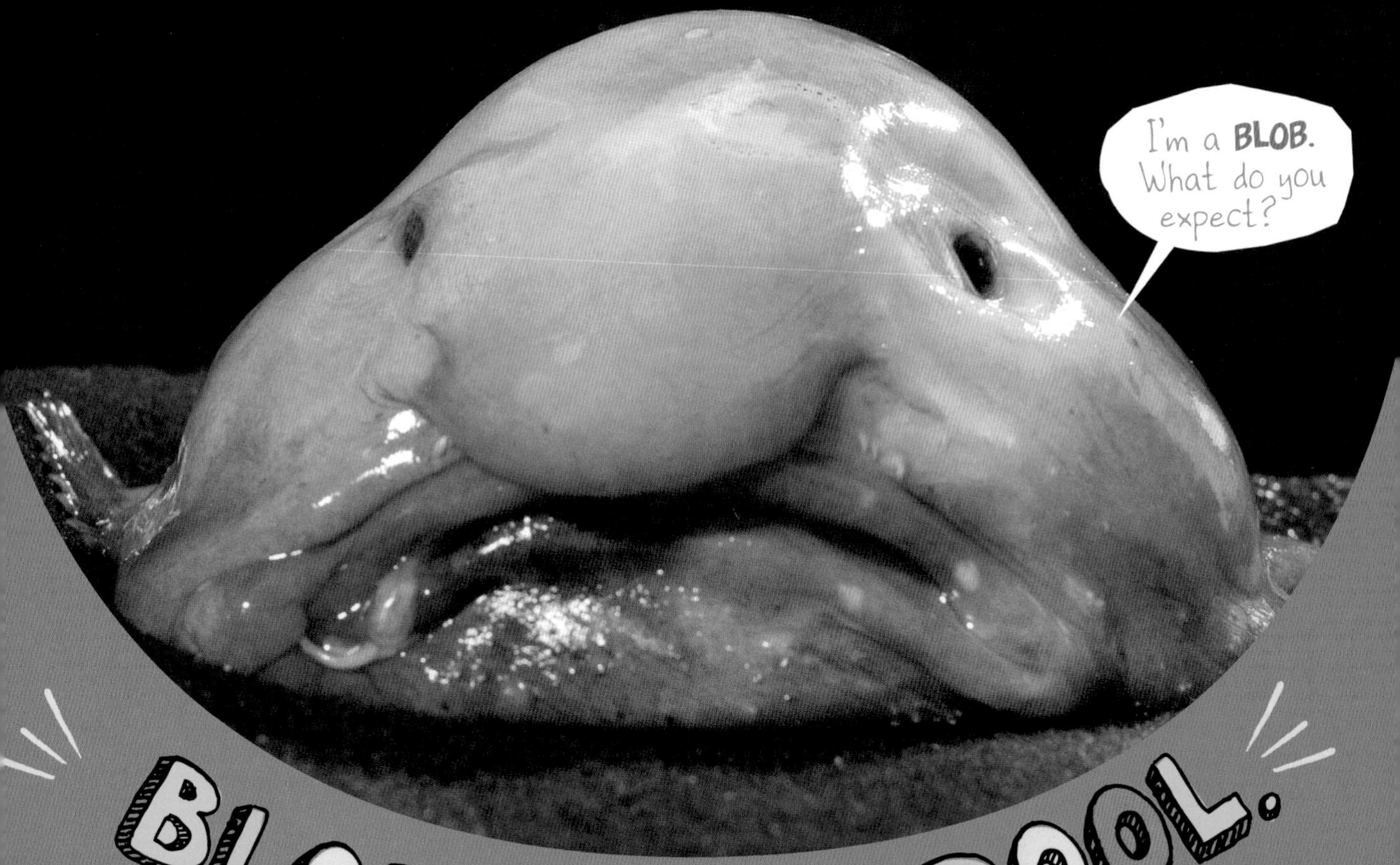

I'm a **BLOB.** What do you expect?

BLOBFISH DROOL.

THINGS FOUND IN SHARKS' STOMACHS:

people's limbs

a bottle of wine

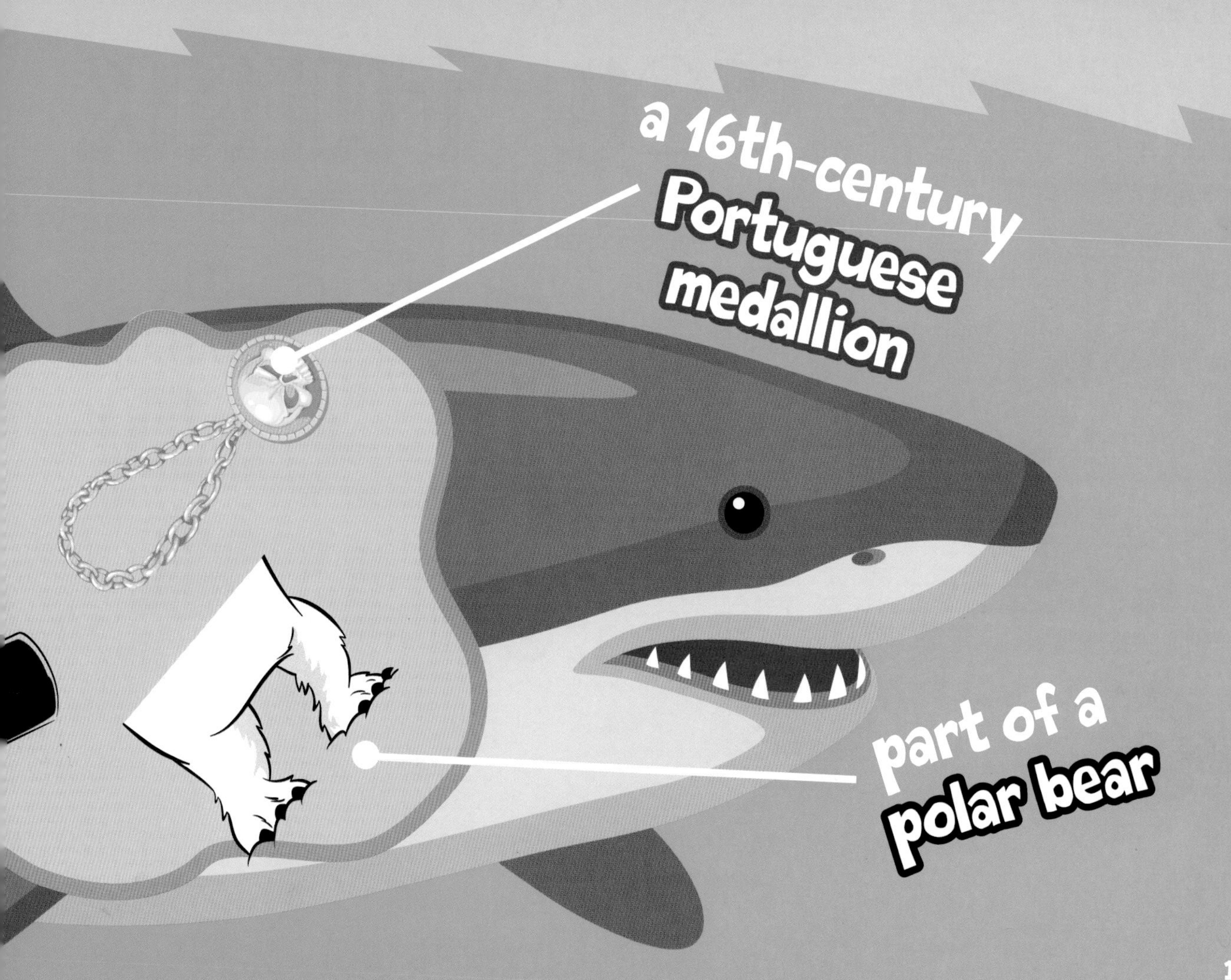
a 16th-century
Portuguese
medallion
part of a
polar bear

YOU THINK

Jellyfish are actually JELLIES.

THESE ARE FISH?

Starfish are really SEA STARS.

When a **colossal squid** swallows prey, the food enters its **brain** before its **stomach.**

A WALRUS' MATING CALL SOUNDS LIKE A BELL RINGING.

The oyster toadfish sounds like A FOGHORN.

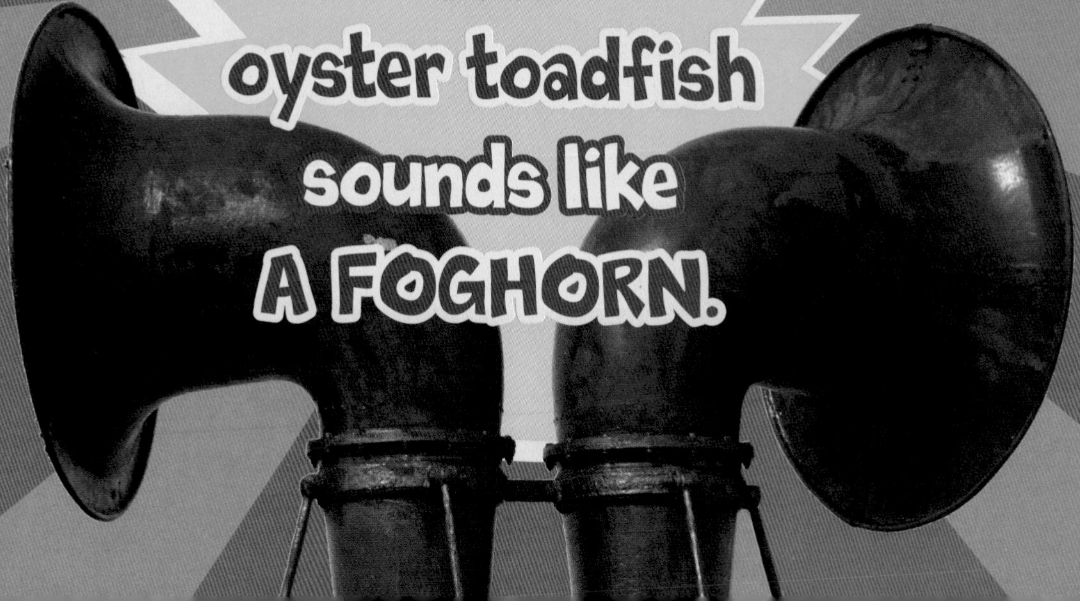

Penguins SING
to each other.

Walruses turn PINK when they get really HOT.

PEOPLE turn pink too!

Cuttlefish can change color to match their surroundings.

Sea otters
HOLD HANDS
while sleeping.

ORCAS slap the water's surface to make waves that push animals off the ice. Then the orcas feast!

AN ORCA IS SOMETIMES CALLED A **KILLER WHALE**, BUT IT'S ACTUALLY A **LARGE DOLPHIN**.

AN ORCA DOESN'T **CHEW ITS FOOD.**

A MANATEE'S INTESTINES CAN BE AS LONG AS THREE AND A HALF SCHOOL BUSES!

Yep, that FITS IN HERE!

The poison
in one
pufferfish
can kill
30 people.

A FEW MINUTES: THE TIME IT TAKES FOR THE TOXINS FROM A BLUE-RINGED OCTOPUS TO KILL A PERSON

Parrotfish eat coral and poop SAND.

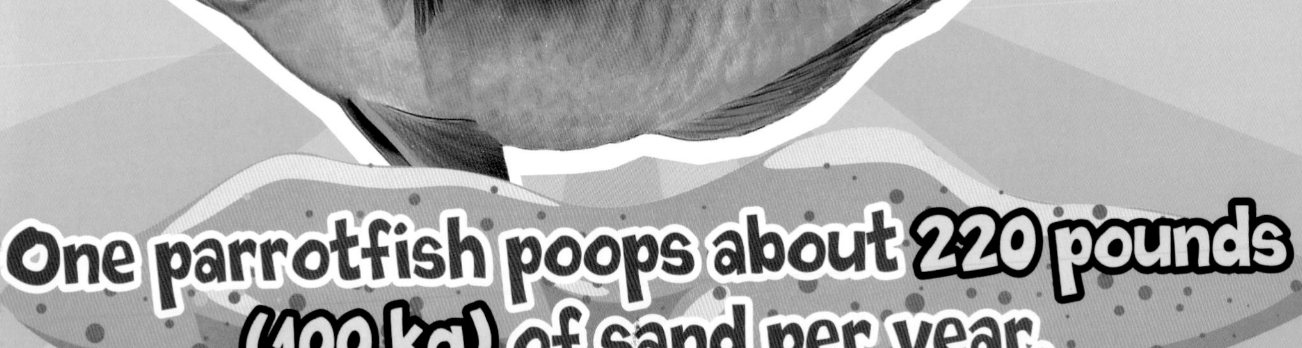

One parrotfish poops about 220 pounds (100 kg) of sand per year.

SEA FLATWORMS
POOP OUT OF
THEIR MOUTHS.

Fish blood?
YUM!

Sea woodlice attach themselves to a fish's tongue, then suck out its BLOOD.

A great white shark has about 300 teeth!

A DRAGONFISH HAS TEETH ON ITS TONGUE.

A dolphin's tooth has **growth rings** that show its age.

A NARWHAL'S TUSK IS REALLY A TOOTH THAT GROWS THROUGH ITS LIP.

Can I SLEEP now?

A POLAR BEAR ONCE SWAM FOR NINE DAYS BECAUSE IT COULD NOT FIND AN ICE FLOE TO REST ON.

Sea turtles lay their eggs on the **same beach** where they hatched.

Humpback whales travel more than **10,000 miles (16,093 km)** in one year.

A clingfish uses its pelvic fins to stay attached to rocks in crashing waves.

SLEEPER SHARKS

SUCK UP FOOD FROM THE OCEAN FLOOR LIKE A VACUUM.

A leafy sea dragon's slurping snout sucks up SEA LICE.

HERRING SCHOOLS CAN INCLUDE **TENS OF MILLIONS** OF FISH.

The largest sea star is 2 feet (61 centimeters) across. The smallest sea star is about ½ inch (1.3 cm) across.

When a sea star eats, its **STOMACH** pops out of its body!

SOME SEA STARS HAVE 40 ARMS.

SOME SEA STARS EAT WHATEVER THEY CAN FIND—EVEN DEAD PENGUINS.

A blue whale EATS 40 million krill in one day.

A great white shark can eat a seal in 10 bites!

A SPERM WHALE EATS ABOUT 20,000 SQUID IN ONE WEEK.

Scientists have seen a living **FRILLED SHARK** only a handful of times.

NO ONE HAS EVER SEEN A GIANT SQUID EAT.

WOULD YOU EAT THESE FOODS?

- [x] calamari (squid)
- [x] soda made from eel parts
- [x] tuna eyeballs

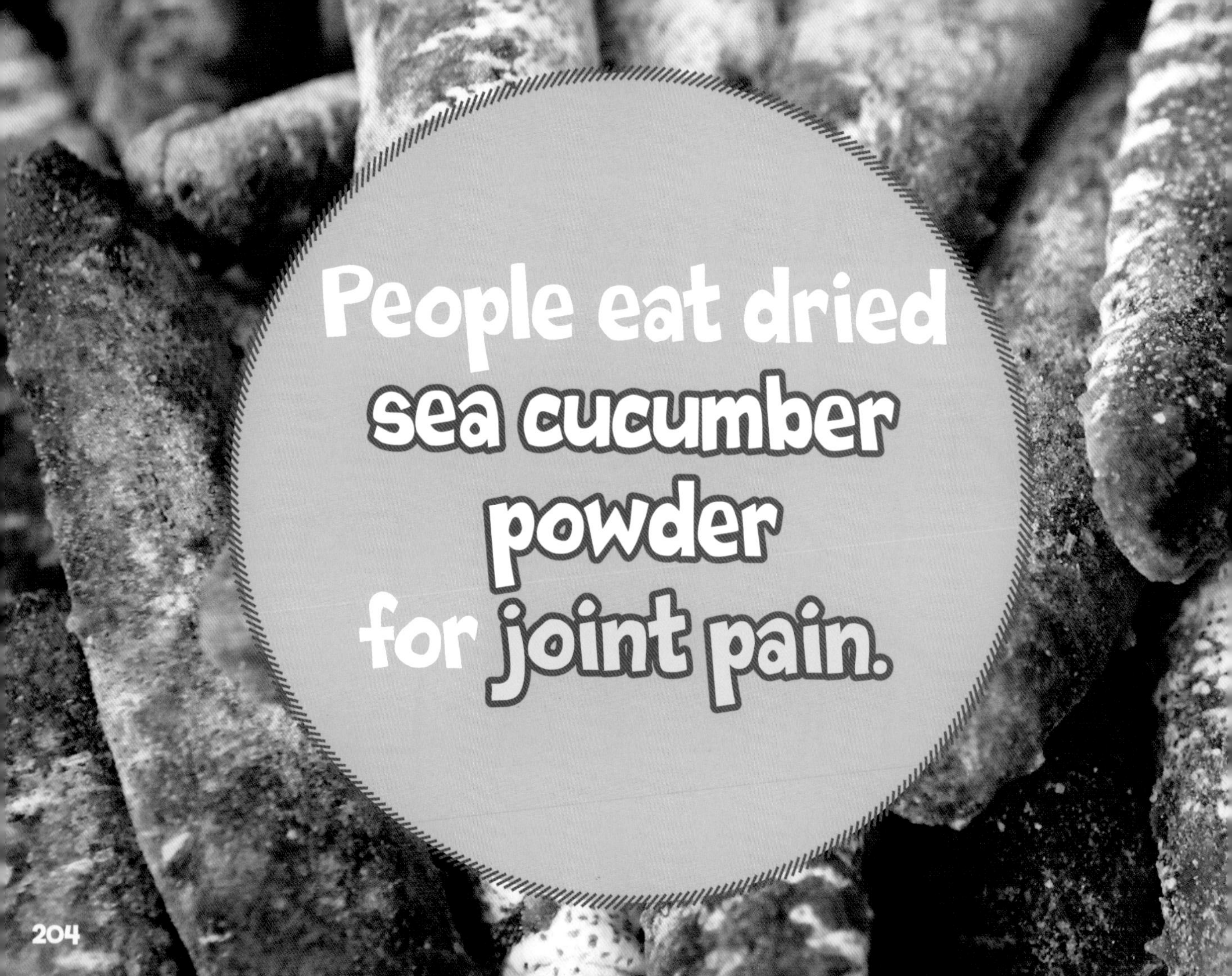
People eat dried
sea cucumber
powder
for joint pain.

The venom in a **box jellyfish** can stop a person's heart in just

30 SECONDS!

A GIANT OCTOPUS CAN DROWN A FULL-GROWN ADULT.

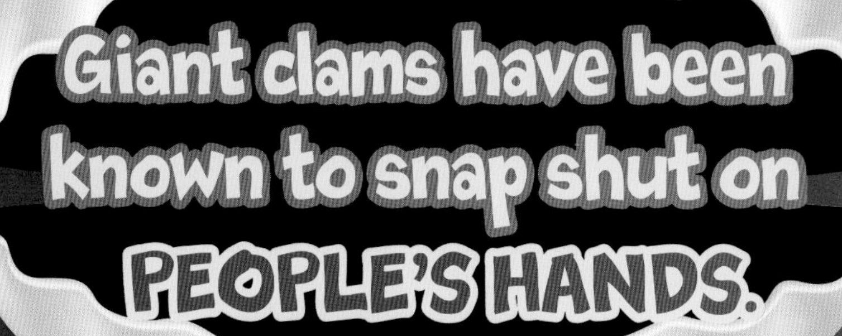

A walrus
can stay
awake for
84
HOURS.

Dolphins sleep with one eye open.

SOME SEALS NAP USING HALF OF THEIR HEAD AND ONE FLIPPER TO STEER.

LOOKING FOR SOME COLORFUL CREATURES?

parrotfish

sea anemone

CHECK OUT THIS CREW!

Christmas tree worms

sea slug

Dolphins toss jellyfish into the air with their heads.

Orcas
PLAY
with their
food.

SHARKS HAVE NO BONES. THEY HAVE CARTILAGE.

But I'm one **TOUGH** dude!

SHARKS SINK IF THEY STOP SWIMMING.

HUMANS ARE A SHARK'S BIGGEST ENEMY.

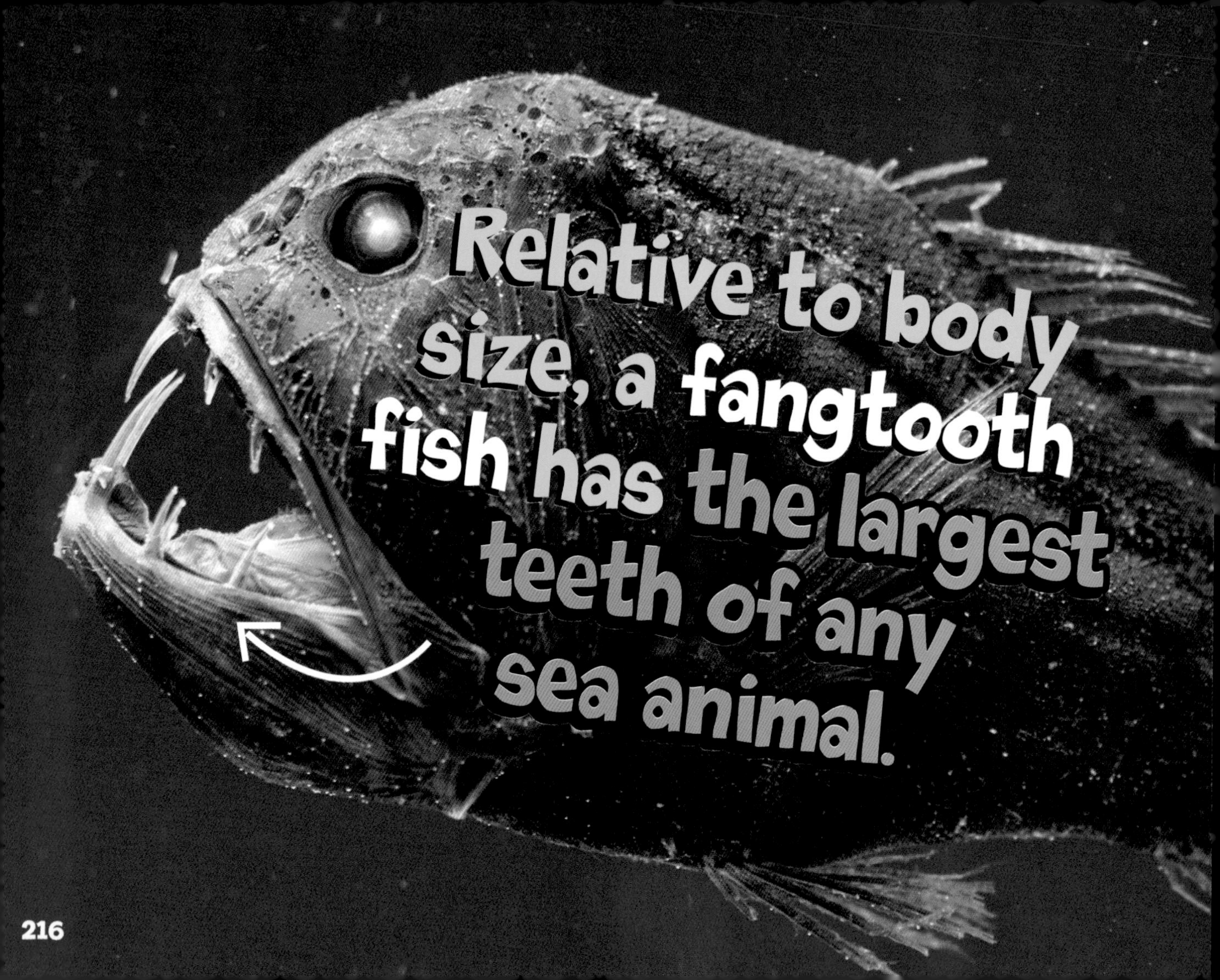

Relative to body size, a fangtooth fish has the largest teeth of any sea animal.

A walrus' teeth can break through 8 inches (20 cm) of ICE.

The stargazer fish can give passing creatures an electric shock.

PEEK-A-BOO!

THE GIANT ISOPOD CAN BE 16 INCHES (41 CM)—THE LENGTH OF A SMALL BASEBALL BAT.

GIANT TUBEWORMS

Some anglerfish are the size of a 3-year-old child.

A dumbo octopus
can live at
depths of
13,000 feet
(3,962 m).

Despite its **GINORMOUS** size, the basking shark eats tiny plankton.

YES, THESE ARE

brain coral

flamingo tongue snail

REALLY ANIMALS!

sea urchin

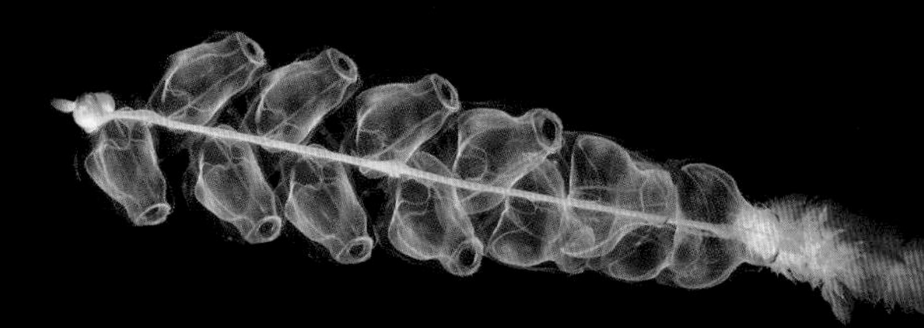

Marrus orthocanna

Why is everyone in such a HURRY?

THE SEA HORSE IS THE **SLOWEST FISH IN THE SEA.** IT TRAVELS ABOUT 0.01 MILE (0.02 KM) PER HOUR.

AMBON SCORPIONFISH HAVE MASSIVE "EYEBROWS."

JELLYFISH ARE 95% WATER.

A WALRUS' EARS ARE INSIDE ITS HEAD.

A lamprey has circular rows of teeth.

A moray eel's throat jaws come up out of its mouth to **grab victims.**

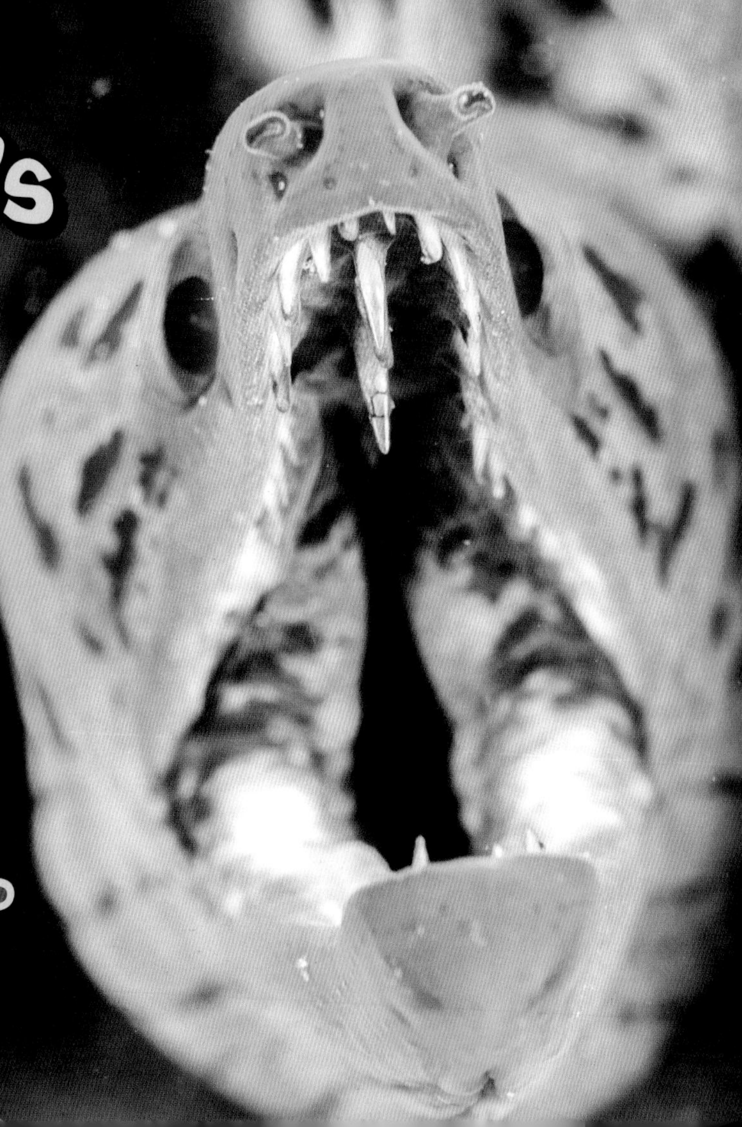

Greenland sharks are so slow, they have to sneak up on sleeping seals **to catch dinner.**

Can you **SEE ME?**

Flounders bury themselves in sand, then ambush their prey.

GLOSSARY

attract—to pull something toward something else

barbel—a whiskerlike feeler on the heads of some fish

cartilage—a strong, rubbery tissue that connects bones in animals

chemical—relating to the basic substances that make up all materials

dorsal fin—a fin located on the back

frequency—the number of sound waves that pass a location in a certain amount of time

gender—the state of being male or female

harpoon—a barbed spear used to hunt large fish

ice floe—a sheet of floating ice

infection—an illness caused by germs such as bacteria or viruses

infrared—one of the colors of the rainbow that we can't see; infrared is next to red in the rainbow

intestine—a long tube that carries and digests food and stores waste products

isopod—an animal that has seven pairs of legs, three main body parts, and a hard outer shell

krill—a small, shrimplike animal

land mine—an explosive device laid on or just beneath the ground's surface

mammal—a warm-blooded animal that breathes air; mammals have hair or fur; female mammals feed milk to their young

medallion—a piece of jewelry shaped like a medal

migrate—to move from one place to another

mimic—to copy

mine—a small explosive device buried in water or in the ground that is set off when a person steps on it or a vehicle moves over it

pellet—a mass of undigested hair, fur, and bones vomited up by an owl

pelvic fin—each of a pair of fins on the underside of a fish's body

pistol—a small handheld gun

plankton—tiny plants and animals that drift in the sea

predator—an animal that hunts other animals for food

repellent—a substance that is able to keep something away

species—a group of animals with similar features

tentacle—a long, armlike body part that some animals use to touch, grab, or smell

uncanny—beyond what is normal or expected

venom—a poisonous liquid produced by some animals

wattle—extra skin that hangs from the head or neck

ABOUT THE AUTHOR

Cari Meister has written more than a hundred books for children, including the "Tiny" series (Penguin) and the "Meet the Monsters" series (Stone Arch Books). She has received many awards for her books. Most recently, "Airplane Adventure" (Stone Arch Books), was named to "Parents" magazine Best Books for 2010. Today, Cari lives in the mountains of Colorado, with her husband, four boys, two horses, and one dog.

LOOKING FOR MORE TOTALLY WACKY TRIVIA?

Available from Capstone
www.capstoneyoungreaders.com

INDEX

Mind Benders are published by Capstone,
1710 Roe Crest Drive, North Mankato, Minnesota 56003
www.capstonepub.com
Editor: Shelly Lyons
Designer: Aruna Rangarajan
Media Researcher: Svetlana Zhurkin
Creative Director: Nathan Gassman
Production Specialist: Lori Barbeau

Library of Congress Cataloging-in-Publication Data
Meister, Cari, author.
Totally wacky facts about animals / by Cari Meister.
pages cm.— (Mind benders)
Summary: Ages 8-12.
Summary: Grades 4 to 6.
Summary: "Presents more than 200 facts about animals"-- Provided by publisher.
Includes index.
ISBN 978-1-4914-6525-7 (paperback : alk. paper)
ISBN 978-1-4914-6535-6 (eBook PDF)
1. Animals—Miscellanea—Juvenile literature. 2. Children's questions and answers.
I. Title.
QL49.M5425 2016
590.2—dc23 2015018533

Photo Credits

Alamy: Dante Fenolio, 220, National Geographic Image Collection, 140; Corbis: Science Faction/Norbert Wu, 157, Visuals Unlimited/David Wrobel, 122; Dreamstime: Daniel Caluian, 43, Ew Chee Guan, 186, Izanbar, 193, Joan Egert, 16 (left), P L, 3, Peter Bjerregaard, 89; Getty Images: Awashima Marine Park, 200—201, Claus Meyer, 30—31, Dante Fenolio, 25, 223, David M. Schleser, 29, Merlin D. Tutle, 17 (top), The LIFE Picture Collection/Bob Landry, 7 (right); iStockphoto: Pedre, 231; Minden Pictures: Mark Moffett, 26, Masahiro Iijima, Nature Production, 54, Norbert Wu, 216, Tsuneo Nakamura, 146, Vincent Grafhorst, 34—35; Newscom: imagebroker/FLPA/Andrew Parkinson, 153, Photoshot/NHPA/Franco Banfi, 199, Photoshot/Oceans-Image/Linda Pitkin, 224, WENN/ZOB/CB2/Karen Gowlett-Holmes, 158, Zuma Press/Caters News/Kerryn Parkinson, 165; Shutterstock: 578foot, 185, abeadev, 7 (left), Abraham Badenhorst, 44—45, abracadabra, 191, Adam Gryko, 39 (frog), agongallud, 109 (top), Alexandra Rachisan, 114 (middle), Alhovik, 4 (party hat), Alice Mary Herden, 6 (right), Amanda Nicholls, 144—145, Amesan, 91, ANCH, 90, Andrea Izzotti, 218—219, Andy Dean Photography, 5, aquapix, 210 (left), Azuzl, 167 (medallion), basel101658, 114 (right), bcampbell65, 211 (left), BDMPhoto, 112, Bildagentur Zoonar GmbH, 106, bluedarkat, 4 (bottom), BlueRingMedia, 66 (bottom), bumihills, 63, Cathy Keifer, 72, cbpix, 133 (left), 214—215, Christian Musat, 178—179, Cosmin Manci, 113, Dave Pusey, 115, Dayna More, 100 (right), dedMazay, 78, 124, 212, Dn Br, 24, Dominique de La Croix, 188, Dr. Morley Read, 92—93, Edwin Verin, cover (bottom left), 100 (left), egg design, 27, Elena Yakusheva, 208, elnavegante, 16 (right), Eric Isselee, 37, 41, 62, Ethan Daniels, 183, fenkieandreas, 232, fivespots, 70, ForeverDesigns, 139, fractalgr, 202, Frank Wasserfuehrer, 103, Fred Goldstein, 176—177, Giovanni de Reus, 167 (bear), Grigory Kubatyan, back cover (right), 173, Hal Brindley, 174, Hung Chung Chih, 14 (right), Iakov Filimonov, 66 (top), Ilya D. Gridnev, 160—161, ingret, 11, Jiri Vaclavek, 168, Jiripravda, 192, Jo Crebbin, 13, John A. Anderson, 125, John Michael Evan Potter, 83, Jon Beard, 47, Kitch Bain, 163 (left), KKimages, 116, koi88, 60, koosen, 17 (bottom), Kristina Vackova, 228—229, Kuttelvaserova Stuchelova, 86, lendy16, 95 (bat), Leonardo Gonzalez, 194—195, LiliGraphie, 6 (frame), lineartestpilot, 68 (middle), Lisa Yen, 68 (right), littlesam, 211 (right), lkeskinen, 162, Lonely, 155, lumen-digital, 53, makar, 88, Mana Photo, 131, mart, 64, mary416, 204—205, Matt Jeppson, 76—77, Matt Knoth, 169, Matthew Cole, 23 (left), Max Fat, 28, Maxi_m, 108 (right), maxicam, 111, mayakova, 69 (popcorn), Memo Angeles, 166 (body parts), mhatzapa, 166 (bottle), Michael C. Gray, 99, Michael G. McKinne, 2, Michael Rosskothen, 198, mountainpix, 74—75, Nagel Photography, 10, NatalieJean, 227 (left), nattanan726, 15, NinaM, 40, nitrogenic, 233, Noradoa, 50, orlandin, 154, panbazil, back cover (left), 4 (top left), panda3800, 4 (top right), PandaWild, 22 (left), Paul Tessier, 110, pcnorth, 87, Peter Waters, 12, Philip Bird LRPS CPAGB, 80, Photo Africa, 55, photobar, 20, photoiconix, 84—85, Phu Hong Phu, 207 (left), pichayasri, 184 (bottom), Polly Dawson, 119, pukach, 164, R. Gino Santa Maria, 206, ra2studio, 207 (right), Radu Bercan, 94, reptiles4all, 22 (right), Rich Carey, cover (top right), 133 (right), 184 (top), Robert Eastman, cover (top left), 6 (left), Ron Rowan Photography, 104, Rozhkovs, 42, 222 (left), Ruslan Mamedov, 226 (left), Sarah2, 19 (top), schab, 112 (tissue), schankz, 35, Sean Pavone, 128, Sergey Skleznev, 210 (right), Sergio Schnitzler, 8, Shane Gross, 134, showcake, 39, Simple Concept, 170, Sphinx Wang, 136, Spreadthesign, 166—167, Stephen Lew, 56—57, 213, Stephen Rees, 172, stockphoto mania, 69, Stuart G. Porter, 117, Sylvie Bouchard, 121, Takashi Images, 132, Tania Zbrodko, 138, Terry234, 108 (left), Tobias Arhelger, 196, Tom Bird, 61, Tony Campbell, 82, tororo reaction, 126, Tory Kallman, 127 (right), tratong, 65, tsnebula23, 71, Vaclav Volrab, cover (bottom right), Vadelma, back cover, 4 (sunglasses), Vadim Petrakov, 14 (left), Valentyna Chukhlyebova, 150, 190, veroxdale, 59, Vilainecrevette, 226 (right), Volkova, 23 (right), voylodyon, 101, wawritto, 96—97, Wayne Johnson, 180—181, whiteisthecolor, 222 (right), Wiktoria Pawlak, 114 (left), Yusak_P, 68 (left), Yusran Abdul Rahman, 137; SuperStock: age footstock, 67, Mark Conlin, 130, Steve Bloom Images, 49, Stuart Westmorland, 163 (back); U.S. Navy Photo by Photographers Mate 1st Class Brien Aho, 143; Wikimedia: Ingo Rechenberg, 33, NOAA/California State University, Monterey Bay/Kevin Raskoff, 227 (right)

Design Elements by Capstone and Shutterstock

Printed in China.
032015 008869RRDF15